CHALLENGED

Mission Trip Devotions & Journal

LENA WOOD

Published by Braughler Books, LLC

Copyright © 2008

Reprinted by permission of Christian Standard Media

Printed in the United States of America

Scripture taken from the HOLY BIBLE, NEW INTERNATIONAL VERSION®. NIV®. Copyright © 1973, 1978, 1984 by International Bible Society. Used by permission of Zondervan. All rights reserved.

Song "Sermon in Shoes" on page 5 from *Living for Jesus* (Vacation Bible School Songbook, 1961, Standard Publishing). © 1952 in *I Know a Joy* by Ruth Harms Calkin. Harmony House, P. O. Box, Pomona, CA.

Lyric on page 77 from "Alrightokuhhuhamen." Words and music by Rich Mullins. Copyright © 1989 Edward Grant, Inc.

ISBN 978-0-7847-2285-5

Braughler™
Books
braughlerbooks.com

A SERMON IN SHOES

You've accepted the challenge for missions, and you're on your way!

Interestingly, the word *challenged* comes from the root *calumnia*, meaning "a false accusation." A challenge, therefore, is a demand for identification, for truth, as in a *challenge* to defend one's honor, or a *challenge* to prove supremacy in sports. Your mission may challenge you to redefine yourself. This experience may reveal new truths, expose weaknesses, uncover hidden talents, cultivate new courage, alter relationships.

You may already have been challenged by financial or time constraints, even the objections of family members. You've met those challenges and won. More challenges lie ahead.

Whether you have a handful of days or a few months at your mission destination, consider a tip for physical, emotional, and spiritual health: wear yourself out.

You've probably heard it said, "Better to burn out than rust out." A wise option somewhere between burning (disintegration) and rusting (stagnation) is to wear out. Your challenge is to wear yourself out for God. Like favorite everyday shoes, be sturdy and of good comfort. Support and protect the ones around you. Try to be a good fit with your on-field leaders. Plan to come back a bit scuffed, stretched, and rain-soaked . . . your soul worn down in spots.

To help you along the way, this journal can serve as a maintenance kit with some spiritual buffers for the challenges you'll face. Included are:

- Glimpses of missionary life and work from all over the world
- Scriptures for meditation
- Helpful tips on travel, culture, and prayer
- Lined pages with each devotion for writing your thoughts and prayers
- A blank page each day for sketching or mini-scrapbooking

An old song by Ruth Harms Calkin, "Sermon in Shoes," says:

Do you know, O Christian, you're a sermon in shoes?
Do you know, O Christian, you're a sermon in shoes?
Jesus counts upon you to spread the Gospel News;
So walk it, and talk it,
Live it, and give it,
Teach it, and preach it,
Know it, and show it,
A sermon in shoes.

We're pulling for you. Stay buff, stay polished, and if you can, stay out of the rain. You've been **Challenged**! Face the challenges and go for it in God's power.

NOTE: Some of the names and locations mentioned in this book have been changed, and the details of some stories represent compilations.

ROUGH AIR

My first mission flight ever was from San Francisco to Japan, the roughest flight of my life. We went over the Japan Alps and into a storm at night, through what is euphemistically called "rough air." That air batted around the plane and its occupants (total weight, a ballpark 800,000 pounds) like a beach ball . . . slamming us down, lifting us, slamming us again. And again. Terrifying.

TRAVEL

If you were encouraged to learn a few foreign words for your trip and have failed to do so, and if you're sitting on a plane right now, here's your chance. Reach into the seat pocket in front of you. That little bag will tell you how to say *puke* in several languages. It may come in handy if at sometime on your journey you can't keep those chunks of mystery meat down.

Though my next few flights were smooth—no rough air—the fear of what I'd experienced crept back in by degrees. Flying is the safest way to travel; we all know that. But the claustrophobic seating, the orange alerts and x-rays at the airport, the 400 mph at 30,000 feet in minus 40 degree temps with a total stranger at the controls . . . seems a tad unsafe, doesn't it?

Within a few years, my fear of flying had reached phobic levels. What to do? Time for a little self-talk.

Me (to myself): *OK, this is getting out of hand—like your arachnophobia. You need to face your fear. Analyze it. What are you afraid of?*

Myself: Dying . . . and maybe the pain before death. Yeah, the pain, the death.

Well, despite the reassuring statistics, it could happen: a deadly air crash. What are you going to do about the fear?

(long pause, like several weeks)

I said what are you going to do?

Face my fears. I guess that means I have to . . . plan on dying?

Now we're getting somewhere. You have to get ready.

I'll pay bills, update the will, hug everyone, tell them I love them.

And . . . ?

And get my heart right with God: confession, repentance. Tell him everything.

What else?

You can't mean . . . ?

Yeah.

Actually look forward to it!?

You do love Jesus, don't you? Believe in him?

Of course.

He lived, died, and rose from the dead to prove there's nothing to fear. You're eternal. You believe all that?

(uncomfortable pause)

I say I do. I'm just not feeling it.

Need to feel it . . .

OK, your turn. Got any fears about the trip? Jot them down below, and face them honestly.

9

The Lord Is

I started reciting Psalm 23 while waiting for takeoff. I thought deeply on it.

The Lord—

Stop there. Who is the Lord?

He's my creator, the almighty one. The Lord is—

OK, stop. He IS. He's the ever-existing one. He IS with you now.

Got it. The Lord is my—

Yes, he's yours. He belongs to you, lives in you. He loves it that you belong to him.

Cool. The Lord is my shepherd—

Stop. David suggests that the almighty God wants to reach down, as it were, and take you—a slow-witted, smelly little sheep—in his arms?

Wow. I shall not be in want.

Exactly. You have everything you need: ticket, seat

belt, wallet, backpack, water bottle, teeny airplane
pillow, oxygen supply . . . and him.

That's all I need.

That's it.

Even if I die.

If you die, you can forego the oxygen and so on. You'll
just have the shepherd.

Ready for Takeoff

After a few runway meditations on Psalm 23, I'm
no longer afraid to fly. I look forward to it, cool with
either destination—Boston or Heaven, Dublin or
Heaven. In the same way, you can look forward to
_____ (your port of call) or Heaven.

When someone sits down next to me with a
weak smile and starts fiddling with his seat belt, if
he snatches a flight magazine and flips nervously
through it without looking at the pages, I sometimes
ask sympathetically, "Don't care for flying?"

"Not really," he'll say grimly.

"I used to be afraid. Now I just plan on dying. You
can't imagine how it helps."

I tell him about Psalm 23, that as we career down the runway, I pray up and say, "I'm comin', Lord!" And that wherever I end up, I'm OK with it.

Sometimes the person gives me a look, turns away, and fiddles even more. But other times honesty happens. One lady—returning from her adult son's funeral—gave me a copy of the service bulletin. On the front was a picture of Jesus standing in the clouds, his arms wrapped around a young man. She mentioned how her son had overcome his struggles with alcohol only to have an old buddy draw him back in. She trusted God to be merciful. There was a calm about her—an air of still waters and green pastures.

We might think of Psalm 23 as the Death Psalm, recited at funerals, on death row, or while escaping down the stairs of the World Trade Center. But really it's a song of life—your final destination is in the house of the Lord forever.

PRAYER

Finish the rest of Psalm 23, phrase by phrase, with your own observations. Rough air or smooth ride, you have what you need.

THE BUTTERFLY EFFECT

Have you heard of the butterfly effect? This theory asks the question: If a butterfly flutters its wings in one part of the world, say over London, will that flutter change the weather in another part of the planet, let's say Los Angeles? In other words, can one small action effect change in a significant way, and in turn cause a larger change, and another, and another?

I believe in the butterfly effect. We see all kinds of evidence that the universe works that way. Cancer starts with a few cells going awry. A tiny rudder can change the course of a cruise ship. One word of encouragement can make your day.

The Bible gives us a raft of examples:

- One bite of forbidden fruit corrupted mankind
- One little baby in a basket grew up to free a nation
- One small stone felled a giant
- One little boy's lunch fed five thousand people . . .

Jesus referred to the butterfly effect, but not in those

terms. He called it the faith of a mustard seed (Luke 17:5, 6). Hardly bigger than the period at the end of this sentence—1 to 2 millimeters—that tiny seed has enormous potential.

Another Global Phenomenon

I believe in the short-term missionary effect, which asks the question: Can one willing person doing small acts of service on a mission field change the world?

I've seen it. An overworked native minister stands in his yard and shakes his head in amazement, saying, "I can't believe a college girl from America would sell boxes of Krispy Kreme donuts to fly halfway around the world so she could pull weeds in my yard. I can't believe it!" A few donuts sold in the Midwest encouraged an overburdened preacher in the East.

I believe in passing out flyers just because the missionary asks. I believe that cleaning a stove, painting a hallway, or staying up all night talking to college students can make a difference. I believe in hugging one child or baking one cake for a bereaved family. I believe a big college guy can stretch out his arms to become human monkey bars for orphans . . . and make a difference.

I believe in singing one song, giving one testimony, spending one day at a pagan shrine to pray down the darkness.

One woman with a passion for missions can sit at a computer in the States and connect dozens of missionaries on the other side of the planet.

One man can dig a well and save a village.

One small prayer group can break ancient strongholds.

One dollar a day can save a life.

Think of several more examples of the short-term missionary effect.

By the same token, great damage may be done with one simple act. We see it every day: one stoplight missed, one drink too many, one stinging criticism, one seductive glance.

TRAVEL

Not to put a ton of pressure on you, but your every move may be watched, your every word analyzed. You are representing yourself, your church, your country, your faith, and most importantly, your Lord. So as you travel around the area of your mission, keep in mind that even your littlest actions may be creating a butterfly effect.

God Is in the Details

The quote "God is in the details" is attributed both to writer Gustave Flaubert (1821–80) and to architect Ludwig Mies van der Rohe (1886–1969). In designing a building, attention to the fine points of color, form, and proportion makes the difference between average and artful. The same is true of words. But it's also said, "The devil is in the details." This flip side, assumed to be a takeoff of the first saying, means what? That a big idea that appears on the surface to be workable can be undermined by unforeseen or overlooked details.

In architecture, one miscalculation can mean disaster. In writing, a missed letter or two changes the whole sentence. Such devilish details of the pen are as apt to be hilarious as harmful. Have a laugh at these newspaper headings (from *Squad Helps Dog Bite Victim* compiled by Gloria Cooper):

- Missionary risked dysentery and bigamy in eight day trip to Nigerian villages
- An Italian Sinner will be served at 5:30 PM at the Essex Center United Methodist Church
- Nicaragua sets goal to wipe out literacy

Yes, God is in the details. This is the essence of the short-term missionary effect. He works through you in the little acts of love and kindness, in a quiet prayer. But beware of the devil's details as well: a harsh word, a missed opportunity that could undermine your mission . . .

"If anyone gives even a cup of cold water to one of these little ones because he is my disciple, I tell you the truth, he will certainly not lose his reward" (Matthew 10:42).

"Whatever you do, whether in word or deed, do it all in the name of the Lord Jesus, giving thanks to God the Father through him" (Colossians 3:17).

DWEEBS IN THE
TEMPLE OF DOOM

I remember Dean as a dweeb: a gawky, shy, plain college guy with a girlfriend cut from the same cloth. They were perfect for each other. *Perfect for the mission field*, I thought snobbishly at the time. Which is where they went—somewhere in the jungles of South America. Out of the limelight, where they'd fit in. They probably couldn't have made it in America anyway. Or so I thought.

You'd especially appreciate the irony of this attitude if you saw my college freshman picture. I was no prize heifer.

Twenty-five years later, I was wandering through hundreds of exhibits at a missionary convention when I spotted at a distance . . . could it be . . . Indiana Jones? Wearing his cool trademark grungy leather bomber, khakis, and a tan fedora, Indy was his usual trim, tan, confident self. On the backdrop of the display behind him was a picture of a bush plane. On the table, a glass case held a coiled boa constrictor.

Wait! I thought. *It can't be Indy. He hates snakes!*

I closed in on the dashing adventurer, the scent of Colombian coffee wafting from a steaming pot. And then I knew.

"Dean!?"

He hadn't aged a day—whereas I'd already entered my part-time blonde phase of life.

Drug lords were as common as fleas on a dog where Dean served as a missionary. One time he barely escaped the jungle with his life. The political situation being what it was, Dean had every right not to go back. But he *was* going back.

CULTURE

No countries are without spiritual "temples of doom" where human souls are held hostage or sacrificed to some lower god. In your mission field, oppression and misinformation campaigns may issue from a dictator's palace, a bandit's lair, parliament, temples of false belief, or entertainment studios.

Intense efforts (whether unwitting or overtly hostile) under the lordship of the evil one will try to undermine the spread of the gospel of Christ by all means possible.

More and more we'll be hearing about mission work in terms of undercover, covert, underground . . . crypto-Christians like those in the first century whose aim was to worship and evangelize and try not to get killed doing it. The Voice of the Martyrs (www.perse cution.com) is a great resource for gaining a deeper understanding of persecution worldwide, and of the incredible courage and endurance of millions and millions of the faithful. The Web site provides running headlines from around the world.

True Heroes

It was a startling discovery: the real superheroes are not the Indiana Joneses. They're the plain vanilla folks who endure. If you consider yourself one of the Not Particularly Cool, could it be that a dose of social rejection counts for something? Could those times of being ignored, put down, or shoved around as a youth pay off in vast reserves of emotional stamina and endurance? Those who survive juvenile dweebdom should have *Everlast* tattooed somewhere on their persons. Forget track stars and football jocks. Ex-dweebs are the magna cum laudes of endurance, and they are the stuff from which we create our heroes.

Dean and his wife are my heroes. They're the cream of the crop, the top of the line, the movers and shakers. How wrong I was!

It's true. Underneath the spandex, Spiderman is a pasty Peter Parker who can't hold down a job. Superman is a namby-pamby reporter named—of all things—Clark. RoboCop is just a few scraps of what's left over of Alex Murphy.

Warriors are wimps in disguise. Or is it the other way around?

True heroes endure. They rise to challenges. They can't live normal lives because it's difficult to keep their supernatural powers a secret.

Think of a few more superheroes and their alter egos. Why do we love 'em so?

God adores dweebs. They aren't weighed down by such pesky qualities as arrogance and pride. They don't preen and put on airs. But they exhibit an uncanny knack for surviving in hostile environments. They're ordinary folks who do extraordinary things for God.

Which makes them extraordinary.

Bearing Under

There are several words related to *endurance* in the Bible. There's *abiding,* which means to stay. And then there's *abiding under,* which means to stay even during hardship and pain. There's *bearing,* as in carrying, like the postman carries a mailbag. Then there's *bearing under,* as in carrying the mailbag through rain, snow, sleet . . . and past vicious dogs.

Moses endured in Egypt. "He chose to be mistreated along with the people of God" (Hebrews 11:25).

Jeremiah endured forty years as a preacher. He put up with plenty of abuse. He had precious little success.

Paul said, "When we are persecuted, we endure it" (1 Corinthians 4:12).

Timothy was encouraged to "endure hardship with us like a good soldier" (2 Timothy 2:3).

Dweebs have a lot in common with the Son of God. He was also underestimated and misunderstood. He hated the humiliation at the hands of people who laughed at him, spit at him. But he put up with it. Why? He endured what he hated (the cross) to achieve what he loved (saving the world).

Are you willing to endure what you hate to achieve what you love?

Is there something in this culture you must deal with in order to succeed in your mission? Fill in the blanks—I will endure (what I hate) to achieve (what I love)—based on the mission trip as you see it unfolding (or based on other things in your life so far).

I will endure _____
to achieve _____.

I will endure _____
to achieve _____.

I will endure _____
to achieve _____.

I will endure _____
to achieve _____.

"Let us fix our eyes on Jesus, . . . who for the joy set before him endured the cross, scorning its shame. . . . Consider him who endured such opposition from sinful men, so that you will not grow weary and lose heart" (Hebrews 12:2, 3).

Notice what superheroes achieve by their endurance: initially nothing for themselves, but plenty for the ones they love. Superman saved Metropolis, RoboCop cleaned up the mean streets of Detroit, and Luke Skywalker rescued civilization from the evil Empire. Spiderman stopped a runaway train. Mostly they did it alone. And we love them for it. Young and old alike collect the action figures and watch the DVDs over and over. We relate because we're all closet dweebs: often insecure, inept, put down, bearing up. And deep down we have the power to be more than ourselves.

Dean was always Indiana Jones somewhere on the inside (which means his wife was always Marion Ravenwood!). And there's a hero inside you. You may just need a few trials in the jungle to prove it. In mission work, it's not enough to abide. You have to abide *under*, to endure hardship. (Grab your whip—

you're going to need it!) And if you are working in a resistant country, you may have to keep your supernatural powers to yourself.

PRAYER

Read Hebrews 12:2, 3 again. Talk to God today about this concept of bearing under. Ask him to grow you more into the image of Christ. It's a dangerous prayer because God may allow some opposition to come your way in order to accomplish his will in your life.

GOD IS NOT

Apophatic theology relates to the belief that God can be known to humans only in terms of what he is not. Here's the gist: If God is truly unknowable, any attempt at saying what he actually is falls short. Therefore, we might better know him by meditating on what he isn't.

I don't know who came up with this idea, but one gets an image of a guy in a loincloth, covered with ashes, sitting on a peak in the Himalayas where the air is really, really thin. In this way of thinking about God, you're not denying he exists, but stating that whatever he might be can't be known.

In one sense, God *is* indescribable. So let's go with what God is *not* for a minute.

God is not . . . you. And he's not limited. And he's not a tree or Shiva or an alien from Venus . . . or one of the ascended masters floating above the Gobi Desert waiting to "externalize" on planet Earth. He's not weak or sleepy or stupid. He's not the sky. He's not an artichoke, and he's not a parking lot. He's not . . .

Add a few of your thoughts.

I don't know about you, but this isn't working very well for me.

Perhaps God *is* unknowable.

God Is

On the other hand, the Word seems to tell a different story. Check out these verses and write down a few things we know about knowing God.

- John 10:38
- John 14:6, 7, 20
- John 17:3
- Romans 1:18-22
- 1 Corinthians 13:12
- 1 John 2:3, 13
- 1 John 4:6, 8, 16, 20

In addition to knowing that we can know God, the Word of God is full of descriptive words to help us know what he's *like*. We'll get to those in a minute. I suppose, though, if we had to say who God is in the fewest words, it could be boiled down to: I AM. God told Moses to tell the doubting Israelites, "I AM has sent me to you" (Exodus 3:14). Let's break that down.

"I"

Yahweh is a person, not a force; a being, not a principle; an I, not an it. Since we're made in his image, we get to be an *I* too. Being created like him, we speak, think, love, live, work, create, and recreate. God designed us to be living souls (see Genesis 2:7). Each of the more than 6.7 billion people in the world is a unique *I*, and God loves us every one.

"AM"

God am. That is, he is. He exists. And since he said that you are made in his image, you definitely exist.

(All of this may sound elementary to the point of abject silliness, but you'd be surprised at the number of "great minds" who have their heads together, stewing over the issue. Some have thought about it to the point that they now believe that nonverbal nonthinking nonbeing unknowing is the best state to be in. Or maybe it's . . . *not* be in. Confusing. Perhaps the great minds need to get out more, take walks, get some oxygen.)

Am, the verb of being, includes *was* (existed in the past), *is* (exists now), and *will be* (to infinity and beyond). The Father *is,* and he created us to *be.* That's awesome! But now we've got another indescribable concept—eternity—to think about. You are headed for eternity, Beloved Child of the One Who Was/Is/ Will Be! How does that make you feel?

Knowing God

What the negative theologians may be trying to say is that God is *infinitely* indescribable—which is true. We could never fully describe His Majesty our Lord. Let's give them that much. But the Bible is loaded with verses full of words telling us a ton about who the I AM is. Since God himself gave us descriptive words in Scripture and a lifetime of experiences with him, let's try that route. Using as many words as you can, describe who God is to you. We'll run the alphabet once to prime the pump: Almighty, Blameless, Christ, Deliverer, Encourager, Father, Glorious, Hope, Impartial, Judge, Kind, Love, Majesty, Near, One, Patient, Qualified, Rock, Shepherd, Teacher, Unsearchable, Victorious, Word, eXcellent, Yours, Zealous.

Or you may want to do a God-is-like list. God is like an oak because he is strong. God is like a rollercoaster because he is exciting. This may be a good time to use some blank pages in your journal to make designs or drawings of things that remind you of God's character and qualities.

Paul said, "I know whom I have believed, and am convinced that he is able to guard what I have entrusted to him" (2 Timothy 1:12). "He made known to us the mystery of his will according to his good pleasure, which he purposed in Christ" (Ephesians 1:9).

The work you are doing testifies to what you know: God is not unknowable. The truth about him is simple, beautiful, and easy to communicate on the field—even across language barriers when words are few.

Jesus loves me!
This I know,
for the Bible tells me so.

No one has ever put it better.

COURAGE IN DREAMLAND

As a small child, Deborah was afraid of everything. Her parents couldn't sit her out on the lawn, because she was afraid of grass blowing in the breeze. When the air conditioner came on and blew dust balls across the hardwood floor, Deborah would panic and scream, "Lean! Lean! Lean!" (meaning "Lint!"). Bugs, spiders, bees—anything that crawled or had wings—scared the daylights out of her. She was mortally terrified of dogs and thunderstorms.

Fast-forward a couple of decades. In 2000 Deborah went on a five-week internship to a Communist country we'll call Dreamland. One night while eating dinner, she casually told her teammates, "I could live here." In the days ahead, she'd often weep in prayer for those people so devastatingly lost. She didn't want to leave.

However, once back in the States, she recalls, "It was as though my humanity kicked in full force. I was suddenly in denial about what had happened overseas, how God had broken my heart for those people. I denied that he wanted me to go back for an extended period."

Deborah would resist the challenge for more than two years, though she did lead a short-term team to Dreamland the next year. The Lord affirmed her call again.

"I argued with him the way Moses did at the burning bush," she remembers, "and God's responses were about the same as those he gave to Moses."

The next year, she said, "OK, Lord, I'll go—but not for another five years. First I have to . . . (yada, yada, yada, fill in the blank with a whole string of excuses)."

How about you? Did you resist or argue with the Lord about going on mission? What were your reasons?

A Life-and-Death Decision

Deborah had persistent dreams of the people, some very intense dreams. She says, "In one of the dreams I was in a cemetery with headstones as far as the eye could see. Someone told me that all those people were Dreamlanders who had died without knowing Christ. I woke up crying."

By December, Deborah stopped fighting.

Was she afraid? She says, "Oddly enough—and perhaps because I had fought God for so long—when the time came to pull up stakes, it was not that stressful. I recruited a team of six friends to help me move overseas. That was a good decision; I didn't have to get on the plane by myself."

But a wrenching moment came when her friends left.

Deborah had purchased a round-trip ticket along with the others because it was cheaper than buying a one-way ticket. But now the airline rep couldn't understand that she wasn't boarding with the group. The more she tried to explain, "I'm not going home," the harder it became. She hailed a taxi and cried all the way back, then cried herself to sleep. But in the morning, the tears were done. Deborah was ready to get to work.

TRAVEL

Perhaps this isn't your first trip. If short-term is a calling for you, it's a good time to think outside the box for travel arrangements. Ask other team members and new friends if they've traveled in unconventional ways. (Who knew that a round-trip ticket might sometimes be cheaper than a one-way?) In the 1950s when missionaries traveled by ship, freighters sometimes allowed a few passengers on board (though maybe this wasn't widely known). Missionaries who took advantage of this opportunity not only enjoyed cheaper tickets but also special perks like eating at the captain's table.

There might be special arrangements for those with a military connection . . . buddy passes . . .

Life in Dreamland isn't easy. Most of its citizens live in superstition. The Communist government acknowledges the nation's deep poverty—and advertises it abroad. But while hundreds of millions of dollars of foreign aid pour in, little has been done for the infrastructure. Government officials, however, live in fine houses and drive Hummers.

Women are socially repressed, often beaten by their husbands. Deborah's introduction to one family came when a neighbor sought help because her husband had taken a glass bottle to her; the wound was still seeping blood the next day.

Transformation

Communism, false religion, loneliness, and misogyny weren't the only threats. Months into Deborah's mission in Dreamland, she was calling her pet dog in for the night. Rachel, a young golden retriever-mutt mix, was barking and wouldn't obey. Deborah went out to coax her inside with treats, only to find Rachel in a standoff with a cobra, its head raised, hood spread for attack. Deborah had already lost one beloved pet to illness; if the snake bit Rachel, she'd lose another. (To some singles far from home, a pet may become as dear as family.) With no thought for herself,

Deborah came up behind the dog, no more than four feet from the snake, grabbed Rachel, and ran. Later Deborah discovered that the area had spitting cobras, which can blind their victims. "I thanked God for rescuing me from my own stupidity!"

TRAVEL

For your own protection ask questions about potentially dangerous local plant and animal life.

If you begin to feel ill, tell your host and keep track of symptoms.

In tropical climates, local doctors recognize diseases such as malaria. But the incubation period between exposure and onset of symptoms can be months. Take care to monitor your health on the field in case symptoms crop up later. For example, ciguatera is a poisoning that results from eating certain tropical fish that live mostly in reef waters of the Caribbean and northern Australia. Nausea and diarrhea may occur several days after eating the fish, followed by strange symptoms even later, such as visual disturbances and possible long-term exhaustion.

Other persistent digestive problems could be caused by parasites or amoebas.

If symptoms occur once you've returned home, be sure to tell your doctor in detail about your travels and diet.

As for Deborah's transformation—from terrors over waving grass and dust bunnies to living alone in a repressive and poverty-stricken Communist country, teaching a forbidden gospel, protecting a neighbor from an abusive husband, and confronting a deadly cobra—how did that happen? The answer is in the story. Discuss it with your team.

Here are some of the results of Deb's mission: Two young women and their teen brother have come to the Lord. The elder sister married a wonderful

Christian man; they're expecting their first child. They're witnessing to their extended family. The gospel is spreading. The other sister, a brand-new Christian, stated that she's ready to die for the Lord—a real possibility in Dreamland. She has no fear of officials or of the future. To leave this world means meeting Jesus.

Use some journal space today to express where your strength and courage come from. How do you see your courage affecting those around you?

PRAYER

Choose one person on your mission field who lives with some kind of danger or oppression. Focus your prayers on him or her today. And as you think about courage, meditate on these verses: Philippians 1:14; Hebrews 3:6; Psalm 121; Isaiah 40:28-31.

MISSIONARIES ARE WEIRD

Imagine that you're strolling down the street in your neighborhood one night. At the end of the block, you spy your neighbors, the Smiths, out in the yard and dressed in their jammies. They're yelling and throwing furniture at each other.

Whoa. Weirdness! you're thinking. *What's up? A drunken domestic brawl? Criminy, there goes the neighborhood . . .*

When you get a little closer, though, you smell the smoke and see the flames. The neighbors' behavior doesn't seem bizarre now. It makes perfect sense. In fact, if the Smiths were idling on the porch while the house burned, *that* would be bizarre!

If your host missionaries should occasionally behave a little left of center, please keep in mind that they know about things you don't: local history and spiritual climate, for starters. If they're lifers in a foreign country, they may be out of touch with "normal" American culture. To them, *Desperate*

Housewives are the single moms in the village, and *Lost* is a spiritual condition.

Or there could be something else going on. A missionary's unusual behavior may signal stress. Or burnout. Many mission agencies now have full-time spiritual support staff to deal with this often-suppressed and long-overlooked problem. Those in the caring professions are subject to burnout, whether on foreign soil or at home.

A Stress and Burnout Primer

Generally speaking, stress results from too many pressures and demands. Long-term, unrelenting stress can end in burnout (www.helpguide.org).

The stressed person expects things to improve if she can get them under control. The burned-out one feels emotionally exhausted and hopeless.

The stressed feel like they're going to explode. The burned-out feel empty.

Stressed people tend to lash out and criticize. Burned-out folks detach, become cynical.

Stress feels like you're drowning. Burnout feels like you've dried up.

Stress can kill you. Burnout can make you want to die.

Have you ever experienced either protracted stress or clinical burnout? What caused it? How did you deal with it?

TRAVEL

You don't want to be stressed and add to any tension already present in your host missionaries' day-to-day lives. But distance traveling and abrupt changes in circumstance can cause temporary physical problems, especially with sleep and digestion. Don't skip too much sleep. Get plenty of water, fresh fruits, and veggies if you can.

Prime Candidate

Jesus was a prime candidate for stress and burnout.

Imagine the good citizens of Jerusalem strolling down the street one day, and there's Jesus throwing furniture in front of the temple and yelling about—of all things—*prayer*! Whoa. Weirdness. There goes the neighborhood.

But at this cleansing of the temple (Matthew 21:12-17), Jesus was seeing things others overlooked: the merchandising of worship, widows starving, children demonized, God's spirit of grace crushed under tedious, man-made rules and restrictions. He must have smelled smoke from the very fires of Hell.

If there had been psychologists in his day, Jesus' friends might have recommended a session. (As a matter of fact, Mark 3:20, 21 says that his family thought he was crazy.) The attending counselor might have said, "I had a chat with your friends. And (*clearing of throat*) while your aspirations are admirable, Rabbi, you may be setting unrealistic goals for yourself. Trying to establish a kingdom under Rome's nose and the constraints of Judaic law . . . Pretty ambitious.

"You haven't said, but you must feel trapped. Am I correct that you have no regular income? I see, a hand-to-mouth existence then? What's that you say? . . . Seek first the kingdom and all these things . . . ? Ah, I see. Noble ideas. However, my recommendation is for you to step away from ministry. Why not try carpentry again? Work with your hands, have a steady income. Give it a month and we'll talk again."

How did Jesus deal with the threat of stress and burnout? He ran to the hills. Alone. He engaged in talk therapy with the only one who understood.

Stress Busters

Rx for drowning in stress: "This is what the LORD says—he who created you, O Jacob, he who formed you, O Israel: 'Fear not, for I have redeemed you; I have summoned you by name; you are mine. When you pass through the waters, I will be with you; and when you pass through the rivers, they will not sweep over you'" (Isaiah 43:1, 2).

Rx for drying up in burnout: "O God, you are my God, earnestly I seek you; my soul thirsts for you, my body longs for you, in a dry and weary land where there is no water. I have seen you in the sanctuary and beheld your power and your glory. Because your love is better than life, my lips will glorify you. I will praise you as long as I live, and in your name I will lift up my hands. My soul will be satisfied as with the richest of foods; with singing lips my mouth will praise you" (Psalm 63:1-5).

Write down a favorite Scripture and one other thing that helps you deal with stress.

PRAYER

Take time as a group to encircle your missionaries. Read the above Scriptures aloud. Then lay hands on the missionaries' heads and shoulders and strengthen them in prayer.

CULTURE

Each culture has its own set of burnout triggers: primitive conditions, cold temps, rigid customs, bureaucracy, crowded housing . . . If you're considering long-term work, look objectively at how you'd manage those conditions.

Note to self: If tomorrow marks a week on mission without a break, it's time for a Sabbath.

PS—But hey, there's good stress too. Remember when you were a kid, so excited to play yourself into exhaustion that you gulped down dinner and exploded out the door for another dusty ball game, another hour on the swing set, more callused hands and scuffed knees, the salty taste of sweat on your lips?

At night you slept like a log. That's good "stress."

If it's good stress you're feeling—exhilarated by cultural barriers, challenged by working with strangers . . . if chaos is your comfort zone and the work seems like play—then ignore this devo; it's not for you, at least not for now. Drop this journal like a hot potato and go play!

69

TIME AND SPACE

Have you noticed yet that mission work messes with your personal time-space continuum? If you're tracking with the journal, this is your seventh day on mission. Does it seem as if no time has passed? Or does it seem that you've been away from home way too long?

The last few days before you left for the trip may have hurtled like a runaway train. Then—especially if you had a long trek—the hours may have slowed to molasses. Days and nights can get skewed. At 4 AM you pop awake, then doze off at lunch as a toddler would, only to get the munchies at midnight. One minute energy, the next minute exhaustion.

TRAVEL

Talk about time warp! Ever been on one of those international flights when the sun keeps going down again and again and again over an endless sea? Who knew? There really is a twilight zone!

How have you acclimated to the new space, your whole life crammed into a suitcase? Does it feel like deprivation, or freedom? Are your current accommodations making you miss home, or—and this can be strangely unsettling—have you suddenly realized that you don't miss home at all, even found yourself thinking, *Hmm, I wouldn't mind living here.*

Does one place feel like real life, the other a dreamscape? Take a break and reorient.

Sabbath

Resting one day out of every seven was an ancient societal law. Even before Moses scaled Sinai, cuneiform tablets from ancient Babylon mentioned Sabattu, "a day of rest for the soul." The meaning was taken to such extreme that during one Babylonian festival, the king was forbidden to eat grilled meat, ride his chariot, or change his clothes (*Unger's Bible Dictionary* by Merrill F. Unger). From the beginning, God gave a "day off" based on creation week: "And God blessed the seventh day and made it holy, because on it he rested from all the work of creating that he had done" (Genesis 2:3). I love how Christian songwriter Rich Mullins put it: "He knocked off work 'cause it was Friday night."

Even cultures that forgot the God of creation kept his pattern for emotional and physical well-being. It's common sense.

CULTURE

Does your mission field have a built-in rest time every day, such as siesta or teatime? Follow the lead of your host family in honoring this practice.

When God set the Sabbath law in stone for the Israelites, they were fresh out of Egypt, where taking a break could mean a beating, or death. For God's people, no cooking, gathering wood, no burden-bearing was to be done, so that they might look back at their rescue from oppression, forward to freedom, and upward to their Savior.

Note the Sabbath-related blessings and curses in Exodus 16:23, 24; Jeremiah 17:19-27 and Ezekiel 20:10-26. What details jump out at you?

"They Make Cinderelly Work, Work, Work!"

Time, worry, and guilt—like wicked stepsisters—will dominate us if we let them. How are they treating you right now? Are you frustrated by work delays when people don't show up? If you're in a building, digging, or gardening project, are you worn out and bored—or more fulfilled than you've felt in a long while? If you're multitasking, is each day crammed to the point of exhaustion? Do you often hurry up and wait? Do you enjoy living in the moment, or do you miss your old routine? Write your thoughts.

Must we keep the Sabbath? We are, after all, under grace, not law. "Spend one day with me," our Father and Friend seems to say, "and your life will be better." Do we answer, "Too busy. Catch ya later"? Do we not trust him to provide if we take time to rest?

It's been said, "As the Sabbath goes, so goes the nation." What does that mean to you?

Painting vs. Pastoring

If this is your first "full-time Christian service," or if you are considering missions longer term, there's something you need to know: ministry is like painting a wall that never ends.

A painter estimates a job—for example, eight hours and two gallons for four walls. He starts at sunup. But when the day's over and the paint's gone, the job's done.

Ministry is *not* like that. Consider for a minute:

- How many in any given church need shepherding, and for how long?
- How many in a community need salvation? And how much time is involved in building relationships, praying, and teaching them?
- How many need physical care and food, and how much will it cost?
- How many leaders need training?
- How many emergencies will erupt?

Ministry is like painting a wall that never ends, with an undetermined amount of paint (apparent resources), no time clock (24/7), and unknowns on the horizon. How much more so on the mission field!

Full-timers have to pace themselves, keeping in mind that God has every resource, he operates in eternity—free of time constraints, and he knows what lies ahead.

Jesus said, "The Sabbath was made for man, not man for the Sabbath" (Mark 2:27). One way to handle a day of rest is simply to choose one day a week with the Lord when you don't push or rush. Move slowly, breathe, stretch, nap. Unlike the poor Babylonian king, you have permission to grill out, take the chariot for a spin, and put on fresh clothes. Under grace, Sabbath is less an obligation and more a gift from God, a rendezvous with him, a rest for body and soul.

PRAYER
Read Psalm 92, a psalm for the Sabbath. Speak it aloud as a prayer to God today.

If you feel crammed or compressed by the current time-space continuum, stop. Look back, look forward, look up.

RECALIBRATING

The Fulanis of West Africa (Nigeria) have been Muslim since the fourteenth century.

The Japanese have worshiped the Shinto sun goddess at the Ise shrine since at least the seventh century (www.wikitravel.org).

The aborigines of Australia had no news of Jesus from the mists of time until the late eighteenth century.

What's the history of religion in your mission field?

Why might it be difficult for a person there to turn from old ways to new life in Christ?

Who's a Christian?

An insightful resource for studying missions more deeply is *Anthropological Reflections on Missiological Issues* (off-putting title, great book). In chapter 6 author Paul Hiebert discusses "The Category *Christian* in the Mission Task."

First, let's say your head deacon quits going to worship service and stops reading the Bible. When his family starts worshiping Hindu gods, he does nothing to dissuade them. Is he a Christian?

Now, using Hiebert's contrasting illustration, let's say a man in India—a Hindu—is walking through his village one day and hears a street preacher. As he listens to the story of Jesus, something stirs in his heart, and he responds to the invitation. He goes back home. He doesn't go to church; there is no church in his village. He doesn't read the Bible; it hasn't been translated into his language—and he can't read anyway. He may not go to a Hindu temple anymore, but his family still does. Is he a Christian?

The Hindu man never experienced—can we call it ambient?—Christianity in a culture that encourages biblical truth. Still, what little he knows about Jesus, he accepts. He's moving *toward* God.

Conversely, most Americans have lived in a culture accepting of churchgoing, Bible reading, hymn singing, and worship of Jesus. But is their faith their own? Have some drifted along lukewarmly? Have they veered from the gospel they once embraced? The deacon above seems to be moving away from God and toward "destructive heresies" (2 Peter 2:1-3; see Ephesians 5:6).

Who's a Christian, the Indian man taking baby steps toward Jesus, or the man living in a sort of civilized apostasy? See the problem? Not everyone who looks or even speaks like a follower of Jesus is one. And vice versa. God has the roll book.

These scenarios may clarify two seemingly contradictory verses: "Everyone who calls on the name of the Lord will be saved" (Acts 2:21); and "Not everyone who says to me, 'Lord, Lord,' will enter the kingdom of heaven, but only he who does the will of my Father who is in heaven" (Matthew 7:21). It's about trajectory, which way you're heading.

A Soft Place to Land

I had a conversation with a Japanese John the Baptist (strange clothes, magnetic message), who goes by only his last name: Ikarashi. We discussed at length the slippery slope of converting to Christ in a pagan culture. I asked him, "How can a person ever be persuaded to abandon a belief system so enmeshed with his national pride and family honor?"

Ikarashi got strangely somber. He thought for a long while, then said something along these lines: "If they could understand it (that their ancient heritage was built on myths and false gods), but if they did not know about Jesus first—if Jesus was not there to catch them . . ." He paused again and said sadly, "I think . . . I think . . . they would die."

Imagine it: clinging by your fingernails to a precipice of disintegrating hope in everything you've ever known, until you're persuaded by the Holy Spirit to let go and fall. And fall.

But if Jesus is there to catch you . . .

So as you meet nonbelievers, talk about Jesus *first*, whenever you can!

PRAYER

Whenever it's appropriate during your stay, pray out loud. Kneel before the Lord. Sing his praises. Be a living visual. Then when your listeners feel the ground under their old beliefs give way, God will be a very present refuge, a safe place for them to land (see Psalm 46).

The Launching Pad

Some Muslim converts to Christ say they've come out of satanic darkness. But others testify that they were always worshiping the one true God, however incompletely (*Islam & Christianity* pamphlet by Don Tingle; see Acts 18:24-28).

Most Japanese don't know that their most ancient sacred text, the *Kojiki*, records that in the beginning—before the sun goddess (which all Japanese know about)—there was a heavenly god, or gods. The world was "a chaotic mass, like an ill-defined egg, but full of seeds." Gradually the finer parts became Heaven, the heavier parts earth. Then a divine couple appeared (www.britannica.com). Sound familiar?

Australian aborigine legends indicate common ancestry with all races through a great flood (see Genesis 9:19). It's welcome confirmation to aborigines that they're not to be viewed as primitive, lesser beings, but equal with all humankind (www. answersingenesis.org).

CULTURE

Dig into the history of any culture and you'll most likely find hints of Bible history or of monotheistic worship. It may be a good launching point for a conversation about God.

As for your own faith . . . If your mission experience has caused you to wonder whether you've been veering toward tradition and trends or leaning on family faith, check your trajectory. Recalibrate your course with the Scriptures. Turn back toward Jesus.

TONGUES

Mission work—as you know by now—requires special attention to words.

A young missionary didn't understand the bus signs, so he learned one phrase in the local language to tell the driver, "Please let me off at Third Street." He was one letter off, using *koro* instead of *oro*. He stepped to the front of the bus and mistakenly uttered, "Please kill me at Third Street."

An American in Chang Mai had to find a restroom. Using all the right tones and pronunciation, she spoke to a guy standing at the entrance to an eatery: *"Kaw pai hawng naam?"* Looking confused, he asked back, *"Gluay tawt?"* (You want fried bananas?)

And consider the young man on a mission trip who asked for a *beeg arnj* at a New York City hamburger stand and was met with a blank stare. In his Kentucky "homeland," *beeg arnj* meant "big orange." He wanted a large orange pop . . . or soda, depending on where you live.

CULTURE

Even if you know a foreign phrase perfectly, the native person may not be expecting to hear you speak his language. He may be straining to understand your English and miss the phrase altogether.

To compound the problem, the deep concepts of grace and one all-powerful God that you're trying to explain may be clearly communicated but still sound foreign to the hearts of your people.

Encrypted Gospel

In some countries, it's the clear messages that spell big trouble.

Fresh out of college, Jeremy went to work in a Communist part of Asia. He kept us updated in code—not using the words *Jesus, church, God,* or *pray*—for fear the authorities might trace e-mail messages. (The Communist authorities are right to be worried. People are flocking to Jesus. Underground estimates range from ten thousand to twenty-five thousand a day.)

Since church growth in the U.S. is slow-go to no-show, I was curious and asked Jeremy how this is happening and who's coming to Christ—Buddhists or atheists or who? Here's his e-mail response:

Most I would say are athst, and many bdst here are such for traditional reasons and most actually really don't believe in it. I do know that we are seeing many new believers and fellowships throughout this country. We go to hospitals and see healings. I have talked with people who tell me that they see dem0ns and some say they hear voices and I've pryed for people who say they have them in them as well. I've never seen this before in person in the U.S., but it is very much a real thing here. We pry for these people and they believe and lives are changed. We were at a fellowship and thirty people came forward to believe. While we (ch leaders and myself) were leaving, twenty others kept surrounding us, asking for us to lay our hands on them and heal them.

They hear. They believe. Amazing.

What things of note happened around you today? How are lives changing during your brief time on the field?

For His Glory

Mamelodi, South Africa, a city of 1 million people, was established in 1953 when blacks were removed from the capital and forced to resettle elsewhere. Unemployment is estimated at 40 percent. Nearly a third have HIV or AIDS (some has been spread due to the diabolic rumor that if you sleep with a virgin, you'll be cured). Crime is rampant. High fences topped with broken bottles surround businesses.

Crossroads Community Church in Cincinnati, Ohio, has developed a partnership with Mamelodi's Charity and Faith Church, a group of fifteen hundred, with eight satellite churches totaling five thousand people. Crossroads sent six hundred Americans to South Africa during the summer of 2007: teams for construction, VBS, music, business, etc.

The Americans went to teach *and* to learn: how to depend on God for everything, how to find joy in dire circumstances, how to pray. And how to forgive—the believers there are so gracious to the white race that has treated them miserably.

Maria Seta went on a music team. Her mission was to teach new songs and techniques to these talented folks, then to work with songwriting, keyboard, and dance leaders to share a worship program.

Maria's class of a dozen girls knew enough English to understand. But on the second day a new student came, speaking only Zulu and Sotho. Despite the language barrier, the girl stayed. Maria and her host prayed that the girl might get what she needed from the class, since she cared enough to come.

On the last day the various classes performed for each other. As they gathered for a group picture, the girl came up to Maria, with a friend to interpret: "She wanted to thank you for speaking Zulu during class so she wouldn't need an interpreter."

Maria halted: "What do you mean Zulu? . . . I don't speak Zulu!"

In a moment, the interpreter began to praise the Lord. "He has given you a gift, Maria! My friend clearly heard you speaking in Zulu!"

Maria was overwhelmed by the miracle, but deeply moved with gratitude. "Anything that will bring God glory," she says. "It's for him and about him."

Two thousand years ago, "a crowd came together in bewilderment. . . . 'How is it that each of us hears them in his own native language?'" (Acts 2:6-8).

What miracles have you witnessed firsthand?

Your Mouth, His Glory

Speak about his glory through whatever language means are available: foreign, English, encrypted, or miraculous. It's the message that matters. Nothing less, nothing else.

There are more than 6.7 billion people on the earth, speaking approximately six thousand different languages. God understands every word all at once. Mind-boggling!

PRAYER

Are your words each day—during teaching, building, cleaning, surgery, writing, or witnessing—are they for his glory? Pray that the living Word will speak through you in new ways.

WAR: WHAT IS IT GOOD FOR?

Not to insult anyone's intelligence, but . . . God is good. Satan is bad. People who deny God and worship Satan are in deep trouble and need your help. Got it?

In spring 2008 a handful of important Christian leaders met with the smiling guru of an atheistic, demon-worshiping, global religion. With folded hands some of the leaders bowed and called him Your Holiness.

Atheistic. Demon-worshiping. Global religion. Wow. What about *antichrist* do we not understand?

I'm especially chafed by the whole thing, mostly because fifteen thousand children were bussed in to sit at the feet of this "holy one" and learn his ways.

Spiritual Warfare for Dummies

Spiritual warfare is needed to contend with half-naked savages threatening in several deep voices, but also to contend with smiling, atheistic, global gurus. And sometimes even to contend with sweet little church ladies or seminary-trained scholars. The enemy peers from behind different faces. At one point Jesus had to tell one of his best friends, "Get behind me, Satan!" (Matthew 16:23).

Even "lost causes" can be redeemed. Think of Mincaye of the Waodani tribe (*The End of the Spear*), Nicky Cruz (*The Cross and the Switchblade*), and Saul of Tarsus (*Acts of the Apostles*—no movie yet; read the book). Our commission is to rescue the perishing—neither condemning, condoning, or complying.

Condemning

Jesus didn't come into the world to condemn it (John 3:17). Satan did. On the mission field—confronted with the unfamiliar—it's easy for us to condemn what's different though not necessarily evil. One new missionary found herself wanting to change the church offering containers because they weren't the shiny metal plates she was used to.

Do worshipers dance to God? David did. Do they drink from the same Communion cup? Jesus' disciples did. Have you found yourself turning up your nose at unfamiliar worship customs on your field? Note them.

Condemnation has its place against dangerous, ungodly practices, and for those in authority who blatantly mislead others. Elijah condemned the priests of Baal. Jesus condemned the Pharisees. Paul, Peter, and Jude condemned false teachers in the early church.

But there is such a thing as misplaced condemnation. What about the kindly church lady who hisses, "Those stupid Muslims!" with not a glimmer of concern for their billion eternal souls? It's not loving to blast people who don't know any better. And what about intellectuals who speak of the church in terms of a "rancid odor"? It's not loving to use shock theology to condemn the bride of Christ.

It's wise to apply the book-chapter-verse test. If you can't find a clear, specific condemnation in the Bible, step back.

The role of a priest—and you *are* a priest—is to lead people toward God and away from evil. Preach Christ and him crucified. Don't lose focus. Time is short.

Condoning

To condone is to regard something immoral in a tolerant way, without criticizing or feeling strongly about it. The new definition of tolerance in our U.S. culture seems to be: "Shut up about moral issues."

Observe how the culture you're in tolerates evil, so that when you return home, you might view your own environment with fresh perspective. What do you see?

Complying

To comply is to obey or to conform. It goes beyond
doing nothing; it gives permission. Compliance to evil
is sin. It calls "evil good and good evil" (Isaiah 5:20).
It indicates agreement. It opens the gates to the
enemy's troops while the battle rages. It surrenders.

We become battle fatigued, don't we? We get
rattled by unimportant issues . . . confused . . .
Eventually, we're nodding at evil just to keep the
peace. We buy the lie.

Antichrist for Dummies

The Greek word *antichristos* means "against, or
instead of, Christ." The early church knew about

him. "Every spirit that does not acknowledge Jesus is not from God. This is the spirit of the *antichrist*, which you have heard is coming and even now is already in the world" (1 John 4:3, emphasis added).

Here's the acid antichrist test: What does a person think about Jesus?

Anyone—believers included—who dilutes the divinity, love, holiness, truth, power, judgment, or kingship of Jesus; anyone who even suggests that Jesus is less than the person revealed in his Word; anyone who trashes his holy bride; anyone who smiles at sin; anyone who despises the people Jesus loves . . . should be lovingly exhorted and prayed over. That person has become a casualty of war.

PRAYER
If you've seen such an attitude in someone on your team, drop to your knees and pray for that person now. Pray for yourself too.

The Armor of God

How does one avoid becoming a casualty of war while in the thick of it? Here are some solid tips for spiritual battle:

- Repent. Get clean of all negative spiritual baggage. Settle any grudges with team members. The evil one feeds on hostility, division, and pride.
- Ask for backup, a team of pray-ers who really mean it. Don't go it alone.
- Praise. Before the battle, praise the Father for his supremacy. Count on the name and blood of Jesus. Listen to the Holy Spirit and obey him.
- Use the sword of the Lord. Psalms and Isaiah have been especially powerful for my teams. Let the Lord guide you.
- Thank him for the victories—seen or unseen.
- Testify to what he's done.
- Read Ephesians 6:10-18. If you haven't used all your blank journal pages, sketch out and label the pieces of the armor of God. The mystery

of the armor is simple enough for a fourth-grader. Look at the pieces: the truth, peace, and righteousness of Jesus; faith in him, salvation through him, and the power of his Word. All the pieces are his, and—here's the secret to spiritual warfare—they *are* him! Romans 13:12-14 points out that putting on the full armor of God is putting on Christ!

"Then I heard a loud voice in heaven say: . . . 'The accuser of our brothers . . . has been hurled down. They overcame him by the blood of the Lamb and by the word of their testimony'" (Revelation 12:10, 11).

Go back and read the first paragraph of this devo. Got it?

HEMISPHERE ONE: THE EAST

Three Worlds

The makeup of the word *hemisphere* is *half* plus *circle*. There are only two halves, whether we divide the globe east/west based on the prime meridian, or north/south in relation to the equator. Most of the world's land mass and population—Europe, Russia, India, China, the Middle East, and most of Africa— are in the northern half of the eastern hemisphere. Here also are the birthplaces of the human race and of the three largest religions: Christianity, Buddhism, and Islam.

Two hemispheres, yet we speak of the third world, a term coined during the Cold War as a way to distinguish those nations that are aligned neither with the West (NATO) nor with the East (the Communist bloc). Later, *third world* came to describe developing countries in Africa, Asia, Latin America, and Oceania. Today, a number of third-world categories are made in terms of civil liberties,

gross national income, or freedom of the press
(www.nationsonline.org).

CULTURE

Historically, there seem to be three *religious* hemispheres; and for the sake of the next few devos, this is where we'll settle.

From Bible times, paganism flourished in the East (Isaiah 2:6).

From the Middle Ages onward in the Middle East and Africa, Islam developed its own culture, while tribal religions were well established in the southern tip of the continent.

Christianity successfully expanded to the West: Europe, the Americas, and Australia.

Of course, all that's changing. Culture cross-pollinates these days. Globalization causes shifts and churns. As Eastern religions move westward, Islam migrates north and west into Europe and America. Christianity grows eastward and southward; now Brazil and South Korea are sending missionaries to us in the West! (www.christianpost.com).

Even if going into "all the world" for you meant traveling a mere hundred miles from home, developing a missions mind-set expands one's worldview—and opens the heart. We'll spend today and the next two days looking at the three religious hemispheres: East, Middle East, and West.

Hinduism is the most ancient known religion in the East, flourishing in India for perhaps four thousand years. Other Eastern religions are Jainism, Buddhism, Confucianism, Taoism, and Shinto. Until this century Christianity has not made great strides in the East.

Tradition suggests that one of the first missionaries to the East was the apostle Thomas, to Malabar, India. Believers in that region today are Christian in faith, Indian in culture, Judeo-Syro-Oriental in worship style (www.wikipedia.org).

Do the Christians in your area worship Jesus differently than you? How so?

Spreading the Word

Here's one for the Go Figure files: China leads the world in Bible production.

Google *Bible production* with *China* and you'll get a bunch of sites. Nanjing, China, is poised to become the world's largest producer of Bibles. By 2007, Amity Printing, a joint venture of the British-based United Bible Societies and a Chinese Christian charity, had increased production to 800,000 Bibles a month. The aircraft-hangar-size facility is expected to supply about one quarter of the world's Bibles by 2009. Most are in Mandarin, but to date about

10 million are in 75 different languages, including English, German, Spanish, French, and many African languages (www.amityfoundation.org).

Communist China leading in Bible production . . . Does God have a sense of humor or what?

And from OneNewsNow.com: In India, in the foothills of the Himalayas, not far from the birthplace of black magic Buddhism, plans are underway for Wycliffe Associates to build a new translation-training center.

Currently more than 180 languages in India are without a translation of the Bible. Wycliffe CEO and president Bruce Smith is partnering with Word for All to provide technical and admin support. Their goal is to cut the time for translating the Bible into all Indian languages from the estimated ninety years to eighteen years.

Additionally, missions like the Doulos ship—a floating book fair—are spreading the Word from port to port. And according to joshuaproject.net, 90 percent of the world's people, if they have access to an Internet café, can hear the gospel in a language they understand.

In the cradle of ancient paganism, in spite of poverty, persecution, disaster, occultism, and Communism, the Word of God is spreading like wildfire!

Arachnevangelism

The evil one hates the spreading of God's Word, and pesters missionaries any way he can. As the editorial team for this book chatted with coworkers about their mission experiences, there emerged eerily similar stories from the three hemispheres. From the East:

It was 1970. Because of a cholera outbreak in Japan, Lynn's college team was required to get shots before they went, then boosters in Japan toward the end the summer. As they headed to a primitive campground at a gorgeous lake near Mt. Fuji, Lynn had a severe reaction to the booster. By the time they arrived, she was in agony and nearly paralyzed on one side.

Bunks in the tiny, windowless cabins were large wooden shelves with homemade, straw-stuffed mattresses. The student campers had taken the best ones; Lynn was left to sleep on what resembled an unfortunate scarecrow. Teammate Carolyn helped Lynn into her bunk and left for the evening program.

"Then I saw him," Lynn recalls, "on the wall a few feet away . . . brown and fuzzy, nearly as big as my hand (though I could have been delirious). There I was, alone with my cholera, my scarecrow, and my spider. I couldn't move. I fell asleep thinking, *Lord, I'm coming home*, and was truly surprised to wake up the next morning. In spite of that experience, it turned out to be a wonderful week in a beautiful mountain setting, sharing Jesus with the campers."

That yucky night was a boot-camp event to teach dependence on God in all circumstances. Lynn would later go on to full-time mission work in Japan. There would be rats under the house, giant centipedes in the shower, icicles dripping from the kitchen faucet, and demons literally breathing down her neck. Still, a small price to pay for ten years of the deepest friendships, a church established, and the most satisfying accomplishments of her life.

Read about one of Paul's missionary journeys in Acts 13. What trials and blessings did Luke write about?

Have you encountered trouble when you talk about Jesus to others? How do you stay strong?

HEMISPHERE TWO: AFRICA AND THE MIDDLE EAST

Africa is the second largest and second most populous continent (900 million) after Asia. There are fifty-three countries, including the island groups. The religious demography is hard to nail down because of constantly shifting political situations, the AIDS pandemic, famine, and wars. But one stat is nothing short of spectacular: In 1900 there were a few million Christians on the continent. A hundred years later, estimates vary but ChristianityToday. com places the figure at more than 400 million.

Sub-Sahara

Explosions are messy events; so is the gospel explosion in sub-Saharan Africa. Early attempts of white missionaries were beset with cultural misunderstandings, greed, patronizing attitudes, and power struggles; and among African evangelists—contentions between prophets and bishops, church splits, visions (false and real), hatred of Europeans, spiritism, polygamy, and persecution by Islam.

We know the name David Livingstone. But who has heard of the "African Apostles" of the 1800s and 1900s: Simeon Nsibambi, Apolo Kivebulaya, and others? What about Christianah Olatunrinle or Charlotte Manye Maxeke? (*Christian History*, Issue 79, 2003). Their influence on the African church was off the charts.

Christlike faith in Africa—despite all strikes against it—has survived and thrived! The dramatic spiritual shift toward Christianity has put Africa in the crosshairs of the evil one. He is losing ground and targeting them. Believers, therefore, must exhibit great courage and tenacity.

In Senegal, the son of a village priest obtained his father's permission to be baptized, but was afraid that if he went into the river, he would die. So he chose a "safer" option: he was lowered by ropes into a 180-foot well, the only place in the area with enough water to be immersed. "If I die, I die," he decided. "I must do all things to follow my God" (*Southeast Outlook*, 01/16/07).

In 2000, bandits broke into the home of missionaries to Benin, West Africa, the birthplace of voodoo. The family was forced to lie on the floor at gunpoint as one by one they were taken into other rooms. The terror went on for an hour and a half. They're convinced their survival was a miracle. Earlier that year, their mission board had asked if they wanted to be highlighted for prayer in the national prayer brochure. They were featured—as it turns out—on the very day they were attacked (*Beyond Surrender* by Barbara J. Singerman).

The stories of darkness and light in Africa will make your hair stand on end.

PRAYER

Today, let the Holy Spirit guide your prayers. Who comes to mind? Pray heartily for each one!

Northern Africa

What African people groups heard the gospel on the day of Pentecost (Acts 2:5-12)? And what about in Acts 8:26-39?

Tradition holds that Jesus' young disciple Mark was one of the first missionaries to northern Africa.

The Coptic (native Egyptian) church has held fast through the centuries, but northern Africa is 80–90 percent Muslim today (www.wikipedia.org). As in other areas in the 10/40 Window, missionaries in northern Africa don't often publicly state which countries they work in and must take great care in reaching the unreachables.

CULTURE

For security reasons, be sure to respect the privacy of the missionaries, and follow all precautions. Some don't want their newsletter information copied or e-mailed. Keep in mind that even after you return home, they will still be living under the eye of local authorities. Don't take chances with their safety.

Which hemisphere are you working in? Do you see opportunities as a result of globalization? Do you see hindrances because of hostility?

The Middle East

As of this writing, of the top ten unreached people groups, eight are in the Middle East, particularly nomadic Muslims (www.joshuaproject.net).

Islam is on the rise in certain places (some arguing that birthrate is the main reason), but stories of Muslims having dreams and visions of Jesus are surfacing. Some people come to Jesus in secret, others openly and at great risk. If you have access to the Internet now, check out some stories. If you haven't heard of the 10/40 Window, check that out too.

Is it any coincidence that the most unreached people live in the 10/40 hotbeds of war, poverty, and persecution—a living illustration of what life is like in a place where Jesus is not known and worshiped?

Arachnevangelism

Today Margaret is an editor who faces deadlines and computer viruses. But forty years ago it was typhoid fever outbreaks, and more. One night on the way into the Congo jungle, Margaret was settling into her sleeping bag on the dirt floor of a thatch-roofed hut. A four-year-old missionary child traveling with the team whispered to her and pointed her little finger to something in the darkness. . . .

Two years earlier, Margaret had landed in Nairobi, Kenya, but with insufficient paperwork to get her from that country through Uganda to the Congo. She was ordered to get the next flight out—and would have had to do that, had not missionary Howard C. signed his life away to get her through. On the first night they met a roadblock in Uganda. Gun-toting militiamen warned them of bandits on the road. It was too dangerous to travel, they said. Margaret, two other adults, and three children were escorted to Kampala—and straight into a walled prison. The soldiers locked the gate and left.

It turned out to be true about the bandits and about the prison being a safety measure, but who knew?

So when—two years and several trials later—a four-year-old pointed to a 6-inch tarantula on the dirt floor near her sleeping bag, the exhausted Margaret said dismissively, "Just cover your head. It'll be OK."

HEMISPHERE THREE:
THE WEST

Europeans learned about Jesus even in his own lifetime. Remember the Roman centurion and Pontius Pilate? Italians, most likely. Then at Pentecost others from Europe heard the gospel. Note the specific areas mentioned in Acts 2:5-12, as you did for Africa in the previous devo.

Biblical Asia Minor is today considered Europe, and Paul is the most notable of early missionaries to Europe. In a vision, a man begged him, "Come over to Macedonia and help us" (Acts 16:9). Today read Acts 16. Note how people responded to the coming of Paul, Silas, and Timothy.

Coming to America

Within five centuries of its beginning, Christianity had spread throughout the same Roman world that had tried so hard to exterminate it. Then, according to Kenneth Scott Latourette's *History of Christianity*, it was through Leif Ericson (AD 970–1020) that Christian Europe first reached North America. Latourette lists other adventurers who wanted to sail across the Big Pond with the gospel: Christopher Columbus, Prince Henry the Navigator, and Magellan.

Over the centuries Europeans flocked to the New World. Diseases were introduced—by accident or later as germ warfare—reducing the native population by possibly 80 percent. Some explorers succumbed to the temptation of wealth of the New

World. With slave labor even more money could be made, so Africans were kidnapped to provide cheap labor for mines and plantations. The gospel liberates the lost, but its European messengers were sometimes derailed by sin and circumstance.

Cultures clash. No society is entirely civilized, nor innocent. At some point in time, Europe would have stumbled upon America and brought in its good and its evil. No need to beat ourselves up; we can't rewrite history.

The church in the West flourished and went into all the world. Today you and I are free and prosperous because of the risks Leif Ericson took.

Prosperity can make one static, can send the church into decline. Why do you think this is so? What can we do to remedy this?

No, we can't rewrite the past, but we can help write the future. One way? You're doing it: short-term mission trips to our dear neighbors. Trips like yours bring awareness and (through the Holy Spirit's tug on our hearts) an increasing willingness to go and give, to set out in the spirit of Leif Ericson—through waters he and other missionaries charted for us, to get uncomfortable once more for the gospel.

Arachnevangelism

One blogger put it well: "In Haiti, the Orkin man would die of a coronary." The blogger also warned travelers to "check your cereal bowl before you put in the milk" and then made reference to "soggy remains."

Dale's team had been on two all-night bus rides: first from Tennessee to Miami; then after a flight to Port-au-Prince, Haiti, and four hours of bartering for buses to base camp. Dale remembers Haitian women holding chickens in their laps on the seven-hour ride to St. Louis du Nord. The mission team arrived at 5:30 the next morning, exhausted. Dale set up his rickety cot in a dark, quiet corner and unrolled his sleeping bag.

"I looked up and saw him . . . a BIG spider that

seemed as large as my hand. Suddenly I wasn't sleepy anymore. Just then we were asked who wanted to go help a missionary at an orphanage. I quickly volunteered."

On the third night, without much sleep and beyond bone-tired, Dale prayed, "Lord, I've got to rest. I ask for your protection. If a spider decides to come and visit me in my sleep, I'm in your hands."

I did a little research on spiders of the world. My guess is, the spider in the Japan story was a trap-door spider or a wolf spider. I also read that wolf spiderlings "disperse aerially." Yikes, they can travel by air!?

But aah . . . tarantulas! If Dale had served in South America he might have met, not a Haitian Brown, but the Goliath, which can grow to the size of a dinner plate.

Dinner. Plate.

However, as with other phobias in the top ten— public speaking, vomit, and thunder (uh . . . it's the *lightning* that'll kill you, friends)—tarantulas are not deadly. Actually, their venom is used to treat medical conditions. Yes, Goliath may hurl barbed hairs at you (which can irritate like fiberglass), and he has 1-inch fangs; but his bite is comparable to a bee sting. And even with eight eyes, Goliath has poor eyesight.

I was struck by the parallel. So many of the evils we fear have worse barks than bites, are more irritating than deadly.

The crux of arachnevangelism is this: Yes, evangelism can be scary. Evil—like the Goliath spider—is self-serving and shortsighted. God's agenda is self-sacrificing and eternal. The Lord made humans quite resilient; we're survivors. We have to keep those truths in mind when things go crawling up the wall, over the floor, or across the ceiling at night.

TRAVEL

If you simply cannot work in an area with big spiders, the Arctic region may be calling you. But—global warming update—all that is subject to change. And read up on those billions of arctic mosquitoes before signing on!

Make no mistake: in all three hemispheres,

persecution can be deadly and seems to be on the increase. According to *World Mission Digest*, there have been more than 100 million martyrs in the last century.

When working in hostile places, take care not to *become* hostile; your battle is not against flesh and blood. Always remember this and you'll not lose your godly *agape* love. The atheist and the militant are themselves victims, deceived insurgents dying in a war that's already been won.

PRAYER
Pray for your enemies, whoever they may be.

Back to Jerusalem

We've been to three hemispheres in three days.

Born in the Middle East, the Christian faith spread across the West and has taken hold in the East. A supernatural, God-size movement of Chinese Christians desires to take the gospel full circle. Resilient networks of Asian churches hope to move westward through Buddhist, Hindu, and Muslim strongholds, teaching as they go until the Great Commission ends where it began—in Jerusalem.

"And this gospel of the kingdom will be preached in the whole world as a testimony to all nations, and then the end will come" (Matthew 24:14).

TRAVELING LIGHT

I remember reading many years ago Paul's list of mission hardships in 2 Corinthians 11:23-28: frequent imprisonments, severe floggings, five beatings with thirty-nine lashes, three beatings with rods, one stoning, three shipwrecks, a night in the open sea . . .

Until his conversion he was a classy Roman citizen and a Pharisee—very upper crust. After the Damascus Road epiphany, Paul became a wandering tentmaker, encountering dangers of all kinds. Every plotline of every adventure novel—man against nature, man against man, man against himself, man against supernatural forces—shows up in Paul's experience.

But it was concern for all the churches that mostly occupied his mind. Paul was under constant stress from all sides. "Who is weak," he asked, "and I do not feel weak? Who is led into sin, and I do not inwardly burn?" (v. 29). Working for God essentially ruined "the good life" for Paul, but he kept praising "the Father of compassion and the God of all comfort"

(1:3). After all, what is a cushy "good life" compared to leading others into eternal life in the very presence of love itself, our creator?

And so we press on . . .

The Darkness

Read Acts 9. Paul was called with a bright light and an accusation from Jesus, "Why are you persecuting me?" The challenge: "Get up and go into the city, and you will be told what you must do" (v. 6).

Three days of blindness followed—total darkness—one of those boot-camp experiences with more to come. God told Ananias, "I will show him how much he must suffer for my name" (v. 16).

Paul was healed, baptized, and given a few days to get his bearings. He hung out with Christians, who kept a wary eye on him. Immediately he began to preach in the synagogues: "Jesus is the Son of God!" Believers were astonished and baffled: *What's this? Radical Judaism's intimidator? The devil's advocate— preaching Christ?*

After many days, Christians were convinced of Paul's sincerity. So were the Jews; they determined to kill him. He hid in a basket and was lowered through a hole in the city wall to escape capture.

In Jerusalem Paul encountered the same resistance: Christians didn't believe him; Jews tried to kill him. Throughout his life, Paul would count among his circle of acquaintances doubters, hecklers, betrayers, sorcerers, prisoners, and assassins. This is what God allowed—even predicted—for Paul: a grueling life and a martyr's death.

The Light

Paul also had what he called "surpassingly great revelations" (2 Corinthians 12:7). He was given super-natural gifts. His insights into the nature of Christ and the Christian life were, in the truest sense, inspired.

Who wants to sign up for Paul's life? It's a conundrum. His letters are filled with joy, gratitude, encouragement, hope, and the desire to keep on. As I read that list of trials and tribulations—and Paul's radical unsinkability—I thought, *Whatever he's got, Lord, I want some of it.*

What strengths and abilities did Paul have?

This but Not That

Second Corinthians 4:6-9: "For God, who said, 'Let light shine out of darkness,' made his light shine in our hearts to give us the light of the knowledge of the glory of God in the face of Christ. . . . We are

hard pressed on every side, but not crushed;

perplexed, but not in despair;

persecuted, but not abandoned;

struck down, but not destroyed."

Read all of 2 Corinthians 4. Then write your own poem according to this same pattern:

I am _____, but not

_____.

Is this your next-to-last day on mission? As a
missionary you've been traveling light in two ways:
You've managed living out of a suitcase with only a
few possessions; you've traveled light. And you are
the traveling light, the light going into a dark place.
What has been your experience? Share your thoughts
with God in prayer today.

Traveling Light Map

As a writer of young teen fiction, I was intrigued
by the popularity of the Harry Potter series, and I
read a few of the books. If I could have one of the
magic things that Harry had, you know what I'd
want? The Marauder's Map. It shows where everyone
is. As little dots move across the map, down halls,
and into rooms, the owner of the map can keep
track of everyone. Each dot is named.

Actually, mine would be a little different. I'd
call it the Traveling Light Map, and it would have
a tiny point of light for each missionary traveling
about with God's truth. There'd be little clumps of

159

lights arcing across oceans as teams flew overseas. Other lights would be converging on inner cities, making a nice glow in a dark place. Sending-agency headquarters would appear as fireworks on the map as summer teams spread out across the earth, thousands of points of light going here and there.

When someone came to Jesus, another point of light would magically appear on the map. And another and another. Each time a martyr died for Jesus, his light would glow brightly for a second, turn red, then fade . . . then reappear floating above the map. From the dark spot he left behind, other lights would magically appear.

In God's mind, I guess, there *is* such a map. He knows where each one of us is—even today! He sees who is carrying his light. He knows when one of us falls.

"Our light and momentary troubles are achieving for us an eternal glory that far outweighs them all. So we fix our eyes not on what is seen, but on what is unseen. For what is seen is temporary, but what is unseen is eternal" (2 Corinthians 4:17, 18).

We don't have the Traveling Light Map, so we must fix our eyes on the unseen glory, the face of Christ. Don't end this day without reading 2 Corinthians 4. And travel light, beloved of God.

TRAVEL

Before you go, get addresses and e-mails of new friends. Leave behind anything you can that would be of use to your host missionaries or those they work with. If you're in an under-developed country, this might include all your clothes except what you plan to wear home!

FAR AND NEAR

What a journey.

What are you feeling at this, the end of your journey? Far from finished? Far from home? Far from satisfied? Far from the number of pounds you thought you'd lose? Far from packed?

Tracking the use of the word *far* in the Bible takes one on quite a trek through God's Word: a kind of theology of distance, spiritual and physical. We've grouped the Scriptures according to the meanings of *far,* bolding and italicizing the word every time it appears in these verses. Dig deeper into any verse that speaks to you.

Traveling

"So Abram left, as the LORD had told him. . . . [He] was seventy-five years old when he set out from Haran. . . . [He] traveled through the land as ***far*** as the site of the great tree of Moreh" (Genesis 12:4-6).

"Pharaoh said [to Moses], 'I will let you go to offer

sacrifices to the LORD your God in the desert, but you must not go very *far*'" (Exodus 8:28).

"If I rise on the wings of the dawn, if I settle on the *far* side of the sea, even there your hand will guide me, your right hand will hold me fast" (Psalm 139:9, 10).

TRAVEL

The circumference of the earth is 24,900 miles. You can go only so far from home (12,450 miles) until you start coming back. With air travel, one can reach most places on earth in one twenty-four-hour day. If you have a map, highlight your journey.

Distance

"If your very own brother, or your son or daughter, or the wife you love, or your closest friend secretly entices you, saying, 'Let us go and worship other gods' . . . gods of the peoples around you, whether near or *far*, . . . do not yield to him or listen to him" (Deuteronomy 13:6-8).

"My friends and companions avoid me because of my wounds; my neighbors stay *far* away" (Psalm 38:11).

"My God, my God, why have you forsaken me? Why are you so *far* from saving me, so *far* from the words of my groaning?" (Psalm 22:1).

"Keep falsehood and lies *far* from me; give me neither poverty nor riches, but give me only my daily bread. Otherwise, I may have too much and disown you and say, 'Who is the LORD?' Or I may become poor and steal, and so dishonor the name of my God" (Proverbs 30:8, 9).

"'Am I only a God nearby,' declares the LORD, 'and not a God *far* away? Can anyone hide in secret places so that I cannot see him?' declares the LORD. 'Do not I fill heaven and earth?'" (Jeremiah 23:23, 24).

"Peter replied, 'Repent and be baptized, every one of you, in the name of Jesus Christ for the forgiveness of your sins. And you will receive the gift of the Holy Spirit. The promise is for you and your children and for all who are *far* off'" (Acts 2:38, 39).

"From one man he made every nation of men, that they should inhabit the whole earth; and he determined the times set for them and the exact places where they should live. God did this so that men would seek him and perhaps reach out for him and find him, though he is not *far* from each one of us" (Acts 17:26, 27).

CULTURE

You can be geographically far from someone yet feel near because of love or common purpose. And you can be geographically near to someone yet feel distance because of belief or attitude. Think of examples of both. Now contrast the culture you've been in with your own culture. Think about how the local customs and traditions—not differences in belief—might needlessly keep you far from forming emotional bonds.

Great Extent

"You, O LORD, are the Most High over all the earth; you are exalted *far* above all gods" (Psalm 97:9).

"King David went in and sat before the LORD, and he said: 'Who am I, O Sovereign LORD, and what is my family, that you have brought me this *far*?'" (2 Samuel 7:18).

"A wife of noble character who can find? She is worth *far* more than rubies" (Proverbs 31:10).

"The Lord says: 'These people come near to me with their mouth and honor me with their lips, but their hearts are *far* from me. Their worship of me is made up only of rules taught by men'" (Isaiah 29:13).

"Listen to me, you stubborn-hearted, you who are *far* from righteousness. I am bringing my righteousness near, it is not *far* away" (Isaiah 46:12, 13).

"As *far* as the east is from the west, so *far* has he removed our transgressions from us" (Psalm 103:12).

"If it is possible, as *far* as it depends on you, live at peace with everyone" (Romans 12:18).

"He raised [Christ] from the dead and seated him at his right hand in the heavenly realms, *far* above all rule and authority, power and dominion, and every title that can be given, not only in the present age but also in the one to come" (Ephesians 1:20, 21).

"If I am to go on living in the body, this will mean fruitful labor for me. Yet what shall I choose? I do not know! I am torn between the two: I desire to depart and be with Christ, which is better by *far*; but it is more necessary for you that I remain in the body" (Philippians 1:22-24).

PRAYER

The great extent to which God can bring us, challenge us, and stretch us when we submit to him is worth meditating on. Share your thoughts with teammates and encourage one another in prayer.

Near

During the course of this trip, did you ever feel far from God? When did you feel the nearest to him?

Abram traveled far, Pharaoh tried to keep the slaves from worshiping far, God brought David far (from a sheep pasture to a palace), Israel's heart wandered far from God—though his righteousness was ever near. The Lord scattered them far. Christ is far above any other god. He brought all of us who were far away *near* through his blood. Near to him, near to each other.

PRAYER

You're preparing for takeoff again. You may have a little "rough air" yet to go through before you reach home. The thoughts and prayers of friends back home have kept you near to them, and vice versa. Have you made new friends who are near and dear to your heart now?

If you have a songbook or access to the Internet, locate the words to "Near the Cross," "Near to the Heart of God," or "Draw Me Close." Sing these lyrics to God as a prayer of consecration.

Read Psalm 139:1-18 and commune with him who is ever near.

ABOUT THE AUTHOR

Lena Wood has a lifelong passion for missions and writing. She's been on five short-term trips to Japan, as well as research trips to Ireland, China, South Africa, and Egypt. Lena maintains contact and prayer support with missionaries from all over the world. She's the author of the Elijah Creek & The Armor of God series and is "Adventure Grammy" to six grandsons.

www.lenawood.com

COMPLETE THE SET

Called is the first in the 3-book set of mission devotional journals.

Are you going on a short-term mission trip? Then you've been Called. Prepare with this devotional journal full of travel tips, an overview of world religions, and great stories from those who've been there and done that.

Changed is the last in the 3-book set of mission devotional journals.

You're back home, and you've been Changed by your adventure with God. Where do you go from here? This journal provides 15 final devos on re-entry, with ideas for doing missions from home.

Order your copies at braughlerbooks.com/store